Margin Call

Howard Mahmood

INT. LARGE INVESTMENT BANK TRADING FLOOR - DAY

The frame is filled with the face of PETER SULLIVAN, a 27- year-old risk assessment analyst. He has a Doctorate from MIT and is staring intently into a large bank of computer screens.
An elevator door opens and FOUR HUMAN RESOURCES PEOPLE come out of the elevator carrying large file boxes. They walk down a long glass enclosed hallway that runs the full length of the trading floor. The scope of the floor now comes into frame. There are more computers than can be imagined and several large boards on the far walls that are scrolling thousands of numbers. PETER gives a knowing glance to the guy sitting next to him, SETH BREGMAN, a young analyst in his early twenties.

SETH
Is that them?

PETER
(nods yes)

SETH
Jesus Christ.
The HUMAN RESOURCES people turn and separate into a large glass walled conference room that runs along the floor as almost every person on the floor watches.
SETH (cont'd)
Are they going to do it right there?

PETER
Yeah.

SETH
Fuck me.
WILL EMERSON, sitting next to them, leans back in his chair.

WILL EMERSON
(whispered)
Have you guys ever seen this before?

SETH
No.

WILL EMERSON
Best to just ignore it. Keep your head down and get back to work... and don't watch.

The HR people begin walking out onto the floor looking at a piece of paper in their hand then walking up behind a person and asking their name. It is brutal. The camera follows one

HR woman, HEATHER, with her piece of paper down the hall and into a row of employees, she walks right past the THREE GUYS then stops a bit down from them.

HEATHER
Timothy Singh?

TIMOTHY
Yes.

HEATHER
I'm afraid we have to speak with you.
TIM gets up and walks back towards the conference room with the woman. PETER puts on his headphones and very loud RAP
MUSIC drowns out all other noise and PETER tries to get lost back into the numbers on his computer screen.
The sequence follows the HR people walking around and firing people intercut with PETER just staring at his computer screen. It runs for almost the length of the song until finally the same woman comes walking back down the hall and stops behind PETER and taps him on the shoulder. He takes off his headphones and the MUSIC STOPS. He is shell-shocked.
HEATHER (cont'd)
Eric Dale?

PETER
Excuse me?

HEATHER
Eric Dale?

PETER
No.

HEATHER
Sorry?

PETER
I'm not Eric Dale.

HEATHER
Oh. I'm so sorry.

PETER
He's my boss, he's down that hall.

INT. ERIC DALE'S OFFICE - CONTINUOUS

ERIC DALE is sitting at his desk, he is 52 years old and looks exhausted. He looks out through the glass of his office as she walks over to the door.

HEATHER
Mr. Dale?

ERIC
Yes.

HEATHER
This way.
ERIC walks out the door first.

INT. TRADING FLOOR - CONTINUOUS
They walk along the full length of the trading floor to reach one of the conference rooms. Everyone left on the floor is watching.

INT. TRADING FLOOR MEETING ROOM - CONTINUOUS

There is a more senior looking Human Resources lawyer, LAUREN BRATBERG, already sitting at the table. They all sit and look at each other for a beat.

LAUREN BRATBERG
Well... Mr. Dale I'm obviously sorry that we are here today but these are extra ordinary times as you very well must know.

ERIC
I run risk management... it just doesn't seem like a natural place to start cutting.

HEATHER
I hope you understand that this is in no way personal. A majority of this floor is being let go today.

ERIC
OK
HEATHER
Mr. Dale. Ms. Bratberg is now going to run through the details of what the firm is offering.

ERIC
OK
LAUREN BRATBERG slides across the table a very thick severance contract agreement.

LAUREN BRATBERG

Mr. Dale the firm is offering you six months severance at half your salary. You will keep all unvested options that you currently hold. Health will be extended through that period. You have till tomorrow at...
She looks at her watch.
LAUREN BRATBERG (cont'd)
4:47 to either take the offer or it will be revoked. Do you understand?

ERIC
Yes.

LAUREN BRATBERG
Now, unfortunately Mr. Dale due to the highly sensitive nature of your work here the firm has to take certain precautions for security purposes that may seem punitive in nature. I hope considering your...
SHE looks down at the piece of paper in front of her to fact check.
LAUREN BRATBERG (cont'd)
...over 19 years of service to the firm, you will understand that these measures are in no way a reflection of the firms' feelings towards your performance or your character.

ERIC
I'm sorry??

HEATHER
She's apologizing for what's about to happen.

LAUREN BRATBERG
Your company email, access to the server, access to the building, and your mobile data and phone service will all be severed as of this meeting. This gentleman...

She points behind him and a smallish benign looking SECURITY
GUARD is standing in the doorway.
LAUREN BRATBERG (cont'd) will take you to your office so that you can clear out your personal belongings.

ERIC
What about my current ongoing work? I'm right in the...

LAUREN BRATBERG
The firm has worked out its transition plan and is prepared to move forward, but we appreciate your concern.

HEATHER
We understand that this is very difficult and here is my card. Please contact me over the next few weeks if there is anything that I can do to help you through this transition in your life.

They all stare at each other in silence for several long awkward beats.

SECURITY GUARD
Sir?
ERIC finally stands up and walks out with the guard and back over to his office.

INT. ERIC DALE'S OFFICE

ERIC walks into the office and sits at his desk and begins to clear his things out into a file box. The guard stands at the door. Eventually ERIC'S sympathetic yet still energetic immediate superior, WILL EMERSON comes to the door.

WILL EMERSON
Hey.

ERIC
Will.

WILL EMERSON
I'm very sorry.

ERIC
Are you still alive?

WILL EMERSON
For now.

ERIC
Congratulations.

WILL EMERSON
It's a total bloodbath.

ERIC
I heard.

WILL EMERSON
If there was anything I coulda done, you know I woulda done it.

ERIC
I know.

WILL EMERSON
Well...

ERIC
One more thing... Who was it?

WILL EMERSON
Eric...

ERIC
Was it Rogers?

WILL EMERSON
You know me. I'm not gonna say...

ERIC
Robertson?
WILL EMERSON just looks back at him in silence.
ERIC (cont'd)
That cunt. I knew it. I never should have gone to her last year.

WILL EMERSON
Look it wasn't anyone. It's just bad luck. Right....?

ERIC
Yeah.

WILL EMERSON
Good luck.
They look at each other with respect but do not shake hands as WILL EMERSON starts
to leave the office.

ERIC
Will?

WILL EMERSON
Yeah.

ERIC
You know I was just in the middle of a bunch of shit here that someone should really
take a look at.

WILL EMERSON
Eric, they are telling us that everyone has got to get out of here and leave everything
behind. While we appreciate your concern, this is not your problem anymore. Alright?
Good luck.

ERIC looks straight ahead as WILL leaves the office. He packs up the last of his things, which does not take long, then stands and gets ready to walk out. He looks around and heads out into the cubicle area.

INT. OUTSIDE ERIC DALE'S OFFICE - CONTINUOUS

Outside his office PETER and SETH are standing to say goodbye.

PETER
Eric, I am very sorry.

SETH
Yeah. Did they say what was going to happen with us?

PETER
Jesus Seth.

SETH
What?

ERIC
No, it will be ugly around here for a while but you guys will be fine...

SETH
Well, take care, Eric.
Seth exits.

ERIC
Well, I'll be seeing you around.

ERIC turns and begins to walk out towards the elevator. PETER walks out behind him.

INT. TRADING FLOOR ELEVATOR BANK

THEY both stand there in silence waiting for the elevator, then.

PETER
I just wanted to say thank you.

ERIC
That's not necessary.

PETER
Well it is... You were the person around here that I...

ERIC looks at him and understands. PETER turns around and begins to walk back toward his desk.

ERIC
I know.
PETER turns back and ERIC reaches into one of his boxes and takes out a small key chain portable hard drive and hands it to PETER.
ERIC (cont'd)
I was close to something here... But they wouldn't let me finish it. Take a look.
The elevator doors open and ERIC gets into the elevator. Just as the doors are closing he says...
ERIC (cont'd)
Be careful.
The doors close.

FADE TO BLACK.
FADE IN:
INT. SAM ROGERS' OFFICE - CONTINUOUS

SAM ROGERS, a 57 year old executive, is sitting behind his desk looking out the window. WILL EMERSON gently knocks on the door, enters then sits on the couch.

WILL EMERSON
Well, that was fucking hideous.

SAM ROGERS
It's gonna get worse before it gets better.

WILL EMERSON
Really?

SAM ROGERS
Much.

WILL EMERSON
Got any nicorettes? I'm out of nicorettes, which means I'm gonna kill someone in about 10 minutes... You alright?

SAM ROGERS
My dog is dying.

WILL EMERSON
I'm sorry?

SAM ROGERS

Just spoke to the vet, it's some fucking tumor on her liver. I'm paying almost a thousand bucks a day to keep her alive.

WILL EMERSON
Really?

SAM ROGERS
Yeah... and I don't have a clue what to do about it.
They both sit in silence and look out the window.

WILL EMERSON
Well they're all gone.

SAM ROGERS
How many do we have left?

WILL EMERSON
Thirty-three.

SAM ROGERS
Make sure everyone is out there, I need to say something.

WILL EMERSON
They are ready for you.
WILL leaves SAM in his office. SAM looks as if he may not move, then snaps out of it.

INT. TRADING FLOOR

SAM ROGERS walks out of his office and stands in front of the trading floor that just an hour before had seated 130 people.
Now just thirty-three are scattered throughout the vast mostly empty space. They all look up in silence at him. Long pause, then SAM'S face begins to glow a bit. His posture straightens, he fills up. He speaks slowly at first then builds.

SAM ROGERS
You are all still here for a reason...
Most of this floor was just sent home... forever. We have spent the last hour saying good-bye... they were good people and they were good at their jobs... but you all were better. Now they are gone.
They are not to be thought of again. This is your opportunity. On every floor of this building and in every office from
Hong Kong to London the same thing is happening. Before this is all done 3 of every ten guys who were standing between you and your boss's job are now gone.
That is your opportunity. I've been at this place for thirty-four years and let me tell you that this will not be the last time you go through this. But you all are survivors... And

that is how this firm over 107 years has always continued to grow stronger. So hold your heads high... and get back to work.
He looks out at them then turns and heads back into his office and closes the door.

INT. SAM'S OFFICE - CONTINUOUS

SAM falls into the couch and looks forward in a deflated daze. His eyes no longer believe what he says.

EXT. INVESTMENT BANK BUILDING PLAZA/STREET LEVEL - EVENING

ERIC DALE walks out the front door carrying the file boxes.
There are other people streaming out the door doing the same thing. ERIC stops, turns, and looks up at the building then tries to make a phone call but his phone does not work as it has been shut off by the firm. He looks up to the sky and can't believe his fate. As he looks down he sees a woman,
SARAH ROBERTSON, serious, classically beautiful and dressed in a well tailored power suit with her head down walking into the building. He can't help himself.

ERIC
Robertson!
SARAH does not respond.
ERIC (cont'd)
Sarah Robertson!
This time she looks up. When she sees him she debates if she should stop. She does. He slowly moves a little closer to her, still carrying the slightly tattered box with his personal belongings in it.
ERIC (cont'd)
You shut off my phone???

SARAH ROBERTSON
Eric... I didn't do anything.
They stare at each other.

ERIC
Fuck you.
They look at each other for a longer beat, both a little shocked that ERIC was so openly confrontational. She turns and heads back inside quickly. ERIC drops the phone to the ground and walks away.

INT. TRADING FLOOR - EVENING

Most of the remaining traders are packing up and getting ready to go home or out for the night. PETER is sitting at his desk holding the portable hard drive. SETH is getting ready to leave behind him. PETER stares down at the drive in his hand trying to decide whether to proceed.

SETH
You ok?

PETER
Yeah. Just a little freaked out.

SETH
You want to get a drink?

PETER
Nah, I need to clean up a few things around here.

SETH
Everyone is going out... come on.

PETER
Nah, I'm fine.

SETH
Well, give me a call if you change your mind.

PETER
I will.

SETH
Come on.

PETER
Where are you going?

SETH
The Grand.

PETER
I'll call you when I'm done.

SETH
Be glad, you're still alive.

PETER
I am.

SETH walks out and PETER puts on his headphones, the MUSIC kicks in again. He picks up the portable hard drive, looks around and sees no one, then inserts it into his computer. He has four large screens in front of him and as he begins opening window upon window of mathematical models his face begins to soften and he gets into his comfort zone. The frame is filled with the extremely complex programs and numbers flying by.

HARD CUT:
INT. VETERINARIANS OFFICE ANIMAL VISITATION ROOM - NIGHT

SAM is sitting next to the exam table, his dog is on the table lying down very sedated. They both stare forward.

INT. THE SOHO GRAND BAR - NIGHT

In a locked off shot SETH and WILL are sitting on a couch staring forward. Figures cross frame and occasionally another banker in the group stops to refill his drink with one of the three bottles in ice buckets on the table in front of them.
They are celebrating, but it seems a little forced.

INT. INVESTMENT BANK TRADING FLOOR - NIGHT

PETER is still working on the numbers, although his face starts to carry a more serious look. He is now wearing glasses and the numbers on the screen are reflected in them. The numbers finally stop moving on the screen and then he takes his glasses off and rubs his eyes.

INT. VETERINARIANS OFFICE ANIMAL VISITATION ROOM

SAM is still sitting next to his dog on the exam table.

INT. TRADING FLOOR

PETER is still in front of his computer, he puts his glasses back on, looks at the screen then quickly picks up the phone and dials.

PETER
(to himself as he dials)
Come on, come on.

OPERATOR RECORDING
The number you have called has been disconnected and is no longer in service.

PETER
Fuck.

PETER hangs up the phone. He looks back at the screen. Then picks up the phone again and dials.

INT. BAR - INTERCUT

SETH
Hello.

PETER
I can't hear you.

SETH
What.

PETER
Go outside, I can't hear you.

SETH
Wait... Give me a sec... OK.

INT. BAR HALLWAY - CONTINUOUS/INTERCUT

PETER
Where are you?

SETH
Lugo.

PETER
Are you with Will?

SETH
Emerson?

PETER
Yes.

SETH
I think he's still here. Why?

PETER
You have to go get him, and get back up here.

SETH
Where?

PETER
The office.

SETH
What!

PETER
I'm serious.

SETH
You want me to get our boss's boss out of a club and bring him back to the office at
10:00 on a Thursday night?

PETER
Our boss just got axed, so technically he is our boss, and yes.

SETH
Why?

PETER
Just do it Seth.

SETH
Alright, we'll be there in ten.

**FADE TO BLACK.INT. MAIN TRADING FLOOR- FIFTEEN MINUTES
LATER**

SETH and WILL walk through the door and into the empty main trading floor. The
lights are down and there is a cleaning person vacuuming in the far background. They
walk over to
PETER'S desk.

WILL EMERSON
Hey, look who it is, burning the candle at both ends. There aren't anymore cuts planned
though, so you can stop kissing my ass, honestly I don't even understand what you guys
do.

PETER
Will, I am so sorry to call you back but
I really think..

WILL EMERSON
Don't worry about it.

SETH
Hey.
WILL is a bit drunk but SETH looks at PETER'S face and realizes something is up.
SETH (cont'd)
What's going on?

PETER
Look at this.
SETH comes around and sits at PETER'S desk.
PETER (cont'd)
Eric gave me this file before he left.

SETH
Eric?

PETER
Dale. And he told me he couldn't quite figure it out, then the last thing he says as the doors on the elevator close is `be careful'.

WILL EMERSON
Be careful?

PETER
So I'm obviously a little curious. So I get into it a bit and I realize that all he was missing was...well it's not good.

SETH looks at the screen and starts to scroll through the pages.

SETH
What is he doing here?

PETER
Go to model four, and it makes more sense.

SETH
Oh.
WILL is now paying closer attention, standing over their shoulder.

WILL EMERSON
What is this?

PETER
This is basically everything that we have on our books at any given time. But what Eric was trying to do here is work it for levels of volatility that fall outside the limits of our standard VAR model.

WILL EMERSON
What are those levels.

PETER
Well it's a fairly complicated...

WILL EMERSON
Simplify.

PETER
The volatility boundaries are basically set using historic patterns then stretching them out another 10-15%... roughly.

WILL EMERSON
So what's happening?

SETH
We are starting to test those historic patterns.

WILL EMERSON
When?
PETER starts scrolling back through the last couple weeks on his screen

PETER
Today.

SETH
Tuesday.

PETER
Monday, last Friday, last Wednesday and
Monday.

SETH
Two Fridays ago.

WILL EMERSON
I get it.
SETH scrolls the final page on the graph.

SETH
Fuck me... Once this thing gets going in the wrong direction...

PETER

Yeah...

SETH
It's huge.

WILL EMERSON
How huge?

SETH
The losses are greater than the current value of the company...?

PETER
Projected losses... projected...

SETH
Fuck me.

PETER
Yeah.

WILL EMERSON
Wait, and this is just our floor?

PETER
Yeah...
They all look at each other long and hard.

WILL EMERSON
Where the fuck is Eric Dale?

PETER
I can't find him, they cut off his phone.

WILL EMERSON
What?
WILL starts off towards his office and is suddenly quite sober. PETER and SETH
follow him.

PETER
They turned off everyone's phone who they axed today.

WILL EMERSON
Fucking ruthless. And he's got no other cell?

PETER

No.

WILL EMERSON
How does he not have his own cellphone?

PETER
I tried, it's been turned off.

INT. WILL EMERSON'S OFFICE

WILL EMERSON
I think I have his home number.

PETER
You're going to call his house?

WILL EMERSON
Yes... Do we even know if he's right?
WILL looks at PETER and SETH standing in front of his desk.

PETER
It seems pretty fucking right to me.

SETH
It does.
The phone starts ringing. We never see Mrs. Dale but we can just make out her responses through the receiver.

WILL EMERSON
Hello, Mrs. Dale?... This is Will Emerson calling... I'm fine, thanks. I was wondering if Eric was there?... Yes, we tried but his cell doesn't seem to be working...

(MORE)

WILL EMERSON (cont'd)
Ok, could you have him call me the moment he gets home, the moment he arrives?
Thank you very much.
Will hangs up the phone.
WILL EMERSON (cont'd)
Where the fuck is he?

SETH
Doesn't he have like three kids?

WILL EMERSON
So?

SETH
I'm just saying, would you go home?

WILL EMERSON
I know where he is. You two need to go get him.

PETER
Now?

WILL EMERSON
Yes.
Will writes the address on a piece of paper. Hands it to them.
WILL EMERSON (cont'd)
There will be a car waiting for you downstairs. Get him back here.

PETER
What are you going to do?

WILL EMERSON
I'm calling Sam.

PETER
Fuck me.

WILL EMERSON
Go.

FADE OUT.
FADE IN:INT. SAM ROGERS' CAR-: PM

SAM ROGERS is driving in his car home from the vet trying to stay awake when his Blackberry starts ringing next to him. He looks down at it, then out to the road, then decides to answer.

SAM ROGERS
It's 11:00 at night?

INT. WILL EMERSON'S OFFICE - INTERCUT

WILL EMERSON
I know I'm sorry. I wouldn't have called...

SAM ROGERS
What's the problem?

WILL EMERSON
I think you need to get down here.

SAM ROGERS
What?

WILL EMERSON
Sam...

SAM ROGERS
It's 11:00 o'clock.

WILL EMERSON
I am well aware of the fucking time, Sam.
But you need to see this.

SAM ROGERS
See what?

WILL EMERSON
Well...

SAM ROGERS
Email it to me.

WILL EMERSON
I don't think that is a good idea.
WILL'S last words hang in the air.

SAM ROGERS
I'm on my way.

INT. BACKSEAT OF A BLACK LINCOLN TOWN CAR

SETH and PETER sit in the back of the plush car as it struggles through traffic up town. SETH reaches into his bag and pulls out a large beer in a black paper bag. Their conversation is quiet, as if they are afraid someone might be listening.

SETH
You want one?

PETER
No.
PETER gives him a bit of a look.

SETH

What, we got them on our way to meet you at the office... we didn't know what the fuck
you wanted to talk about...
(almost to himself)
... thought you might've gotten some chick pregnant or something.

PETER
I haven't gotten laid in so long that's not possible at this point.

SETH
I guess that's true.
PETER looks out the window at all the people on the street enjoying the Thursday night.

PETER
Look at these people.

SETH
What?

PETER
We are in here stressing our fucking heads off that the world as we know it is ending,
and they've got no idea what's coming.
SETH'S demeanor sitting and drinking a beer doesn't seem to project much in the way
of stress.
PETER (cont'd)
Right?

SETH
I try not to let work get to me.

PETER
I've noticed that about you actually.

SETH
Look, we are twenty three years old...

PETER
Twenty-Seven.

SETH
Whatever, same thing, I made almost a quarter of a million dollars last year... for what...
pushing some numbers around on a computer screen, so a bunch of glorified crack
addicts could take that information and pretend to understand it, and then make a bet
against some other jock half way around the world who if he wasn't doing this would
probably be in some OTB somewhere putting it all on number seven. And at the end of
the day one guy loses and the other guy wins.

PETER continues to look out the window in silence for a long beat. Then with a little sly humor and a smile to SETH:

PETER
You do know it's a little more complicated than that?
SETH'S phone starts playing a ring tone. He looks down at the text.

SETH
It's Will... He wants to know if we've found him? What do I tell him.

PETER
Tell him that we haven't found him.

INT. TRADING FLOOR

SAM ROGERS comes through the door from the elevator looking quite disheveled and walks across the long and empty trading floor. He looks around, then heads over to WILL EMERSON'S office where the light is on.

INT. WILL EMERSON'S OFFICE-CONTINUOUS

SAM lightly knocks on the glass.

SAM ROGERS
Hey.

WILL EMERSON
Hey.
SAM looks at WILL for some hint of what is going on, then eventually puts his coat down and sits into a chair. They wait for who goes first.

SAM ROGERS
So?

WILL EMERSON
Eric Dale...

SAM ROGERS
Oh Jesus...

WILL EMERSON
Before he was escorted out of the building by security...

SAM ROGERS
I had nothing to do with that.

WILL EMERSON
I know.

SAM ROGERS
I'm sorry, go on.

WILL EMERSON
So as he was leaving the building he hands a disk to Peter Sullivan...

SAM ROGERS
Who's Peter Sullivan again?

WILL EMERSON
One of Eric's guys.

SAM ROGERS
Right.

WILL EMERSON
...and tells him that he was almost on to something but hasn't been able to figure it out. So he gives him the disk and says give it a try... but the last thing he says as the doors to the elevator close is `be careful'...

SAM ROGERS
Be careful?

WILL EMERSON
Yeah.

SAM ROGERS
Be careful?

WILL EMERSON
Yes.

SAM ROGERS
Why?

WILL EMERSON
Well... take a look.

SAM ROGERS
Speak, you know I can't read those fucking things they put together.

WILL EMERSON
Basically the kid dives right into the thing after your little pep talk, nice job by the way, and he seems to have nailed it.

SAM ROGERS
Nailed it?

WILL EMERSON
The kid figured out what Eric was missing. And...

SAM ROGERS
And?
WILL gives him a long pause.

WILL EMERSON
...it isn't good.
WILL'S look gets SAM up and he comes over to stand behind
WILL at his desk and look at the computer.
WILL EMERSON (cont'd)
As far as I can tell these here are the historical volatility index limits... which I guess our whole fucking trading model relies on pretty heavily... and we are so fucking levered up that if this thing starts getting outside those limits it gets ugly in a hurry.

SAM ROGERS
How ugly?

WILL EMERSON
Real ugly.

SAM ROGERS
And how close to those limits have we gotten?

WILL EMERSON
Oh we're beyond close... We broke through five or six days over the last two weeks, but we've managed to stay on the upside of it... for now...

SAM ROGERS
For now?

WILL EMERSON
Well look what happens here when we get on the wrong side of it.

SAM ROGERS
What am I looking at?

WILL takes his finger and points at a red number with a whole lot of zeroes after it.
SAM'S look says it all.

WILL EMERSON
And that wouldn't even be that bad a day for us... historically speaking.

SAM ROGERS
Is this right?

WILL EMERSON
I don't know.

SAM ROGERS
Where is Eric?

WILL EMERSON
We shut his phone off.

SAM ROGERS
Of course we did.

WILL EMERSON
And he hasn't come home yet, I spoke to his wife.

SAM ROGERS
He's probably crying in a fucking beer somewhere.

WILL EMERSON
Or worse.

SAM ROGERS
Where's the kid who did this?

WILL EMERSON
Out looking for Eric.

SAM ROGERS
Do we think he knows what he's doing?

WILL EMERSON
I don't know. What do I know?

SAM ROGERS
Well get him back here.

INT. UPSCALE CABARET CLUB ON THE UPPER EAST SIDE-CONTINUOUS PETER and SETH are sitting at the bar each with a drink facing camera. There are women dancing in the background and one dancing in front of them, PETER and SETH look up occasionally.

PETER
What now?

SETH
We should probably tell Will he's not here.

PETER
Yeah.
They both just continue to look forward and sip their drinks.

SETH
What do you think this girl makes in a night?

PETER
Seth.

SETH
?
PETER keeps looking forward.
SETH (cont'd)
2000? Fuck. That's.... All things considered, that's not bad.
Eventually SETH'S phone starts to ring. He picks it up.

SETH (cont'd)
Will?... No, no, we asked and no one's seen him.
They exchange a look and slam their drinks.

CUT TO:
EXT. THE TOWNCAR IN TRAFFIC

This time they are really stuck in traffic, the car is not moving at all.

INT. BACKSEAT OF A BLACK LINCOLN TOWNCAR

Eventually the car starts moving, and SETH'S phone starts buzzing with a text again.

SETH
He's freaking out. We need to get down there.
They look out into the city. Finally SETH reaches into his bag and takes out the forty in the paper bag and starts drinking the beer again. He takes a big sip.

SETH (cont'd)
What'a you think Rogers makes in a year?
Long pause.

PETER
I have no idea?

SETH
Come on, play along.

PETER
I don't know what year?

SETH
Last year.

PETER
Three quarters of a million bucks?

SETH
Come on.

PETER
What?

SETH
Not even close.

PETER
More?

SETH
Yes.

PETER
A million?

SETH
Will Emerson made two and half million bucks last year.

PETER
Fuck you.
SETH looks at him showing he is serious.
PETER (cont'd)
Fuck you!

SETH
He did.

PETER
How do you know that?

SETH
He told me.

PETER
He just told you that?

SETH
Well I asked him.

PETER
Do you think that's true.

SETH
Probably.

PETER
That's fucked up.

SETH
Why?

PETER
Does that seem right to you?

SETH
Right?

PETER
Jesus.

SETH
So what do you think that means Rogers puts away?

PETER
I have no idea.
They both just look straight forward, SETH takes a big gulp of the beer.
PETER (cont'd)
This fucking traffic. We should have taken a the subway.

INT. TRADING FLOOR ELEVATOR BANK- FIFTEEN MINUTES LATER

The doors of the elevator open and PETER and SETH look up as
WILL EMERSON and SAM ROGERS are standing in front of them about to get onto
the elevator. WILL and SAM are now dressed with fresh shirts, ties, and suits and look
as if they are ready to start a new day even though it is almost one in the morning. SETH
is still holding the forty in the paper bag.
Will looks at it. They share a glancing smile. WILL and SAM step into the elevator
keeping the guys in it.

WILL EMERSON
Gentlemen?

SAM ROGERS
You're coming with us.

SETH
Will. Mr. Rogers.

WILL EMERSON
Sam this is Seth Bregman and this is
Peter Sullivan.

SETH
Sir.

INT. ELEVATOR - CONTINUOUS

SAM ROGERS
Guys.

They all stand in silence as the elevator heads up until:

PETER
Will?

WILL EMERSON
Yes?

PETER
Where are we going?

SAM ROGERS
Going to get a second opinion on your work Peter.

PETER and SETH look at each other, growing more concerned.
The doors open and they exit.

INT. HALLWAY BY JARED'S CONFERENCE ROOM - CONTINUOUS

SETH looks for somewhere to throw out his beer but can't find a trash can. They follow SAM and WILL down a long hallway that is crowded with assistant cubicles. Eventually they turn into a small conference room that has no windows. It is claustrophobic.

INT. JARED'S CONFERENCE ROOM - CONTINUOUS

There are four people sitting at the table. They stand.
Everyone says their somber hellos and shakes hands.

ALL PRESENT
Slight hellos, etc.
They all sit down and at each place setting there is a pad of paper, a pencil, and an empty binder. Sitting at the head of the table is JARED COHEN. He is a blond boyish looking 43 year old, although carries himself with intense confidence.
He is the head of all fixed income securities, and oversees roughly 25,000 employees. Next to him is his chief risk management officer, SARAH ROBERTSON, the same woman from outside the building earlier who had the run in with ERIC.
Next to her is her right hand man RAMESH SHAH, a sixty year old number cruncher and next to him is a firm lawyer. They are all dressed sharply for a new day. Long silence.

SETH COUGHS.
ALL PRESENT look down at him.

JARED COHEN
So Sam, what do you have for us?

SAM ROGERS
Well... it should be here in a minute.
Finding someone in the copy room at this hour was a little bit of a challenge.

JARED COHEN
Well why don't we start by introducing everyone then.

SAM ROGERS
OK.
JARED COHEN
This is Sarah Robertson who you know, our chief risk management officer, Ramesh Shah from upstairs, and David Horn one of the firm's in house counsel.

SAM ROGERS
Nice to meet you all. This is Will
Emerson my head of trading, and this is...

WILL EMERSON
Peter Sullivan, and Seth Bregman. They work in our risk department.

JARED COHEN
Where is Eric Dale?

SAM ROGERS
He was let go today.
JARED COHEN looks at SARAH ROBERTSON as it would have been her call to let
ERIC go, she nods yes.

JARED COHEN
So who's left in your risk department?

WILL EMERSON
As of today that would be Peter and our junior analyst Seth...?
Everyone looks down the table at PETER and SETH. Their inexperience glares back.

JARED COHEN
Really?
JARED looks back at SARAH, then the room goes silent again.
Finally a COPY ROOM STAFFER knocks on the door.

COPY ROOM GUY
Will Emerson?

WILL EMERSON
Here. Please just give one to everyone, thanks.
The COPY ROOM GUY hands out the packets to everyone in the room.

SAM ROGERS
So apparently Eric had been working on this for some time but was unable to finish it,
as he was leaving the building today he gave the program to Peter here, and told him to
see what he thought.
Peter figured a few things out that Eric seemed to be missing and this is what came out.

JARED COHEN
Where is Eric Dale now?

SAM ROGERS

He's been unreachable since he left the office.
JARED COHEN and the others open up the printout in front of them and start reviewing. SAM, WILL, PETER, and SETH just sit in awkward silence staring at the other side of the table as they all read. This goes on for a full very long minute.
Finally:

SARAH ROBERTSON
Peter this is your work?

PETER
Mainly Mr. Dale's...

SARAH ROBERTSON
But this draft is yours?

PETER
Yes. Again, derived from Mr. Dale's original model. But yes.

SARAH ROBERTSON
And what is your background?

PETER
Background?

SARAH ROBERTSON
Your CV.

PETER
I have been with the firm for two years working with Eric that whole time... But
I hold a doctorate in engineering, specialist in propulsion, from MIT, with a Bachelors from Penn.

JARED COHEN
What's a specialty in propulsion?

PETER
Well... in laymen terms my thesis was a study in the way that friction ratios effect steering outcomes in aeronautical use under reduced gravity loads.
Long silence.

JARED COHEN
So you are a rocket scientist?
The whole table looks over at Peter with some awe.

PETER

Um... I was... yes.

JARED COHEN
How did you end up here?

PETER
Well it's all just numbers really, you're just changing what you're adding up... and if I
may speak freely the money is considerably more attractive here.
JARED looks down again at the numbers in front of him and his tone suddenly switches
to serious, testy even.

JARED COHEN
What time is it?

RAMESH
It's 2:15.
SAM and JARED just look at each other in silence for a bit.

JARED COHEN
What do you have in exposure right now, tonight?

SAM ROGERS
I don't know... between 900 and 1.3... roughly.

RAMESH
If Mr. Sullivan's numbers are correct...
RAMESH looks down at the sheet in front of him to go through the numbers and takes
a beat too long.

PETER
1.215 Trillion.
RAMESH checks his number.

RAMESH
Yes.

JARED COHEN
Fuck me... fuck me... And I'm guessing by the fact that you two haven't said anything
that the math checks out?
JARED looks over at SARAH and RAMESH. SARAH then looks to
RAMESH. She looks back.

SARAH ROBERTSON
Look   we'd need a little more time to go over   this, but Mr. Sullivan here seems to
know   what he's doing. And I don't have to tell   you that this is a problem.

JARED COHEN
Thank you for that. What time is it?

RAMESH
JARED COHEN
Fuck me!
Jared stands up and walks around the small room. The rest of the room goes silent.
Finally:
JARED COHEN (cont'd)
Sam how long under normal operations would it take your people to clear that from our
books?

SAM ROGERS
What?

JARED COHEN
The 1.2 trillion.

SAM ROGERS
All of it?

JARED COHEN
Yes.

SAM ROGERS
I don't know, a couple weeks?

JARED COHEN
Weeks?

SAM ROGERS
Yes. But as you certainly know our business is selling AND buying. It doesn't work for
very long without both components. If we suddenly stop buying for a day or two that
just doesn't hide under the rug, it gets out and this whole this thing comes to a end... and
right quick.

JARED COHEN
I understand.

SAM ROGERS
Do you?

JARED COHEN
How many traders do we have left between your floor and Petersen's?

SAM ROGERS
I don't know, sixty.
RAMESH has been looking down at the numbers while this conversation has been taking place.

RAMESH
Jared I've just been looking here a little closer, and it's these VAR numbers that are really setting this thing off.
JARED holds up a hand to interrupt Ramesh. Jared nods his head, his eyes are perfectly still but his brain is racing.

JARED COHEN
Excuse me, I need to make a quick call.
JARED calmly stands up and steps out of the room for a long moment. The room stays completely quiet the whole time he is gone. We hear nothing. It is awkward to say the least. He comes back in and sits down without missing a beat.
JARED COHEN (cont'd)
Please...

RAMESH
I was just saying, and just speaking completely off the record here, it won't be long before someone else starts putting these in and sees the exact same thing we are looking at here. If they haven't already.
Pause.

JARED COHEN
Understood... And Sarah, what value would you allow to be placed on those assets that might be left on the books, if they had to be?

SARAH ROBERTSON
Why would they still be on the books?

SAM ROGERS
Because suddenly no one wants to buy them.

JARED COHEN
Oh fuck you Sam... give me a fucking break, all at once?

SARAH ROBERTSON
Without an active market, it could take weeks, months for me to value them correctly. You'd have to go block by block.

SAM ROGERS
It's a very simple business Jared. You and I talked about this last year...

JARED turns around suddenly and cuts him off.

JARED COHEN
Sam.... Will, Peter, and..??

SETH
Seth.

JARED COHEN
Seth, Could you please excuse us for a few minutes.
They stand up and start to exit the room.
JARED COHEN (cont'd)
Oh and Peter? Who else has seen this?

PETER thinks that through.

PETER
No one... besides us here.

JARED COHEN
And Mr. Dale.

PETER
Yes.

JARED COHEN
And can it really be that we don't know where Eric Dale is?

WILL EMERSON
I'm afraid so. His wife tells us he hasn't come home yet...and the firm shut off his phone today.

JARED COHEN
Perfect. Well, I need to know where he is.
WILL, SETH, and PETER leave the room and close the door behind them.

INT. CORNER OUTSIDE JARED'S CONFERENCE ROOM - CONTINUOUS

They cross the hallway and sit on a bench staring out the window. They talk very quietly.

SETH
Jesus fucking Christ! Who is that guy?

WILL EMERSON

He's Sam's boss.

SETH
He looks like he's fifteen years old. How old is he?

WILL EMERSON
He's like forty.

PETER
How does that happen?

WILL EMERSON
Oh it happens all the time. Except to me.
Kid's a fucking killer.

PETER
What are they talking about?

WILL EMERSON
It ain't pretty.

SETH
What ain't pretty?

WILL EMERSON
If people suddenly stop buying the shit we're selling....
They all look out the window. Long pause.
WILL EMERSON (cont'd)
You guys smoke? Well, you should.

INT. JARED'S CONFERENCE ROOM

SAM ROGERS
Jared you can't do what you are thinking about doing.

JARED COHEN
What if we don't have a choice?

SAM ROGERS
What does that mean? Fuck you... you don't have a choice.

JARED COHEN
Fuck me? Have you looked at these numbers
Sam??

SAM ROGERS
Yes, but what the hell do I know.
JARED COHEN comes back over to the table and picks up the packet.

JARED COHEN
Well, Mr. Shah tell me if I'm wrong but to me these numbers don't add up.

RAMESH
If I may I'd like to take some time before we...

SARAH ROBERTSON
Jared we can't answer that yet.

JARED COHEN
Are you fucking kidding me... this is exactly what we've...
SARAH now cuts him off abruptly.

SARAH ROBERTSON
We need a little time before we can give you our conclusion.
SARAH closes the issue off with another look to JARED.

JARED COHEN
OK. We meet in 45 minutes.

RAMESH
Sam, do you have this file?

SAM ROGERS
Yes, here it is.
SAM slides him the hard drive across the table, they all take a second to follow it.

JARED COHEN
And Sam we need Eric Dale, it's making me very uneasy knowing he is out there right now wanting to put a knife in our backs while he's not even aware he's holding the knife in his hand.
SARAH and RAMESH leave the room as SAM is left alone with

JARED.
SAM ROGERS
What are you going to do?

JARED COHEN
Not sure.

SAM ROGERS

Are you going to call him?
They both look at each other for a long beat. Finally.

JARED COHEN
I already did.
SAM puts his hand on JARED'S shoulder briefly. They part.

   OMITTED
OMITTED

EXT. ROOFTOP - CONTINUOUS

They walk over towards the edge. It is a very clear night.

SETH
Jesus.

PETER
Wow.

WILL EMERSON
Yeah.

SETH
Shit, that's a long way down.

WILL EMERSON
Yeah, it is.
They sit down on a girder, then light up. WILL'S look and tone becomes a little darker
as they all stare out into the night. Long Pause.

INT. JARED'S FLOOR ELEVATOR BANK

SARAH and JARED wait for the elevator alone in silence. The doors finally open and
they get in.

INT. ELEVATOR- CONTINUOUS

Still not a word. Finally.

SARAH ROBERTSON
Is this really where you want to be taking this at this point?

JARED COHEN
I'm sorry?

SARAH ROBERTSON
We don't even know if he's right.

JARED COHEN
How long should this take you to confirm?

SARAH ROBERTSON
Not long.
Silence except for the ding as it comes to the floor and the doors open.

JARED COHEN
OK
They part.

EXT. ROOFTOP - CONTINUOUS

THEY are all still smoking and looking out over the city.
Finally WILL stands up and goes over to the edge and looks over. He jumps up and sits
on the edge.

PETER
Careful.

SETH
Jesus man.

WILL EMERSON
Did you know the fear most people feel when they stand on the edge like this is not
actually a fear that they will fall but instead it's the subconscious fearing that they might
jump? ....It's a fear of losing faith.

SETH
Well that's a little deep and depressing, thank you.

WILL EMERSON
Yeah well, I can get a little dark sometimes.

SETH
Will, come on. Get down.
WILL jumps down and comes back over to sit down. They stare out again.

WILL EMERSON
Not today!
(beat)

So it looks like they are gonna have us dump this shit.

SETH
What?

WILL EMERSON
Yeah, you watch.

SETH
How?

PETER
A trillion bucks??

WILL EMERSON
I'm just saying.

PETER
How would they even do that?

WILL EMERSON
You can't... it's impossible. But they'll figure out a way. I've been at this place for ten years and I've seen some things that you wouldn't believe... and when all is said and done... they don't lose money. They don't care if everyone else does, but they won't. Long silence.

SETH
Will?

WILL EMERSON
Yeah?

SETH
Did you really make two and half million bucks last year?

WILL EMERSON
Yeah... I did.

PETER
What do you do with all that money?

WILL EMERSON
I don't know really. It goes pretty quick. You learn to spend what's in your pocket.

SETH

Two and a half million goes quickly?

WILL EMERSON
Well the tax man takes half of it up front. So now you got what... million and a quarter. Mortgage grabs another 300K, I gave 150 to my parents to live off, so now you got what??

PETER
Eight hundred.

WILL EMERSON
I bought a car last year for 150.
Probably another 100 eating... 25 on clothes, put 400 away for a rainy day...

SETH
Smart. (smiles)

WILL EMERSON
And what's that?

PETER
125 left.
WILL EMERSON takes a long drag off his cigarette.

WILL EMERSON
I spent 76,520 dollars on booze, dancers, and whores.

PETER
WILL EMERSON
Yeah, kinda shocked me, although I was able to write most of it off, as entertainment. With that he flicks his cigarette over the edge of the building just as a massive CORPORATE HELICOPTER comes sweeping up from behind the building and comes right over their heads.
THEY are now YELLING above the rotor noise.

| **PETER** | **SETH** |
| Whoa! | Whoa! |

WILL EMERSON (cont'd)
What time is it?

SETH
:!
WILL EMERSON
Oh, here they go. They are bringing in the cavalry! We better get down there.

INT. JARED COHEN'S CORNER OFFICE - CONTINUOUS

JARED and SAM are sitting in the office silently looking out the window. The office is very large and has a full sitting area with two couches. JARED is intensely going over the papers in front of him. SAM is just looking out the window.

SAM ROGERS
How old are you?

JARED COHEN
SAM ROGERS
Jesus...
JARED stops reading with a deeply aware look and just stares out the window as well.

JARED COHEN
This is a very... very bad dream.
SAM looks over at him directly.

SAM ROGERS
I don't know, seems like we actually may have just finally woken up.
SARAH ROBERTSON comes to the door. SAM sits up.

SARAH ROBERTSON
Hello.

JARED COHEN
Come in.

SAM ROGERS
How do we look?
Her look says it all.
SAM ROGERS (cont'd)
I should go.

SARAH ROBERTSON
No, you should stay.

JARED COHEN
So?

SARAH ROBERTSON
(dead calm delivery)
It's all legit... the kid killed it. The formula is worthless.
They all look at each other as if they have seen a ghost.

JARED COHEN

What do you mean?

SARAH ROBERTSON
It's broken.

JARED COHEN
There are eight trillion dollars of paper around the world relying on that equation??

SARAH ROBERTSON
We were wrong.

JARED COHEN
You mean you were wrong.

SARAH ROBERTSON
Don't even start.... This was discussed.

SAM ROGERS
I'm heading to the conference room.

SARAH ROBERTSON
No.

JARED COHEN
I'd like you to hear this.

SAM ROGERS
No... I don't want to hear this.
SAM stares at them both.
SAM ROGERS (cont'd)
How do you think I've stuck around this place so long.
He walks out of the room. SARAH and JARED look each other over.

JARED COHEN
I've called Tuld.

SARAH ROBERTSON
Is there a contingency plan here?

JARED COHEN
A contingency plan?

SARAH ROBERTSON
Yes.

JARED COHEN
We went all in on this one.

SARAH ROBERTSON
So we've got ourselves quite exposed here... haven't we?

JARED COHEN
To Tuld or the market?

SARAH ROBERTSON
Both.

They both stare at each other. Jared's phone buzzes. He takes it out and his face says it all.
SARAH ROBERTSON (cont'd)
He's here.
His face says yes. Sarah walks out. Jared stands up and straightens his tie in the reflection of the window. He exits.

INT. OUTSIDE JARED'S OFFICE - CONTINUOUS

Tracking shot of Sarah and Jared walking through cubicles.

   INT. FREIGHT ELEVATOR HALLWAY - CONTINUOUS
They cut through a short cut near the freight elevator. WILL,
PETER, and SETH are coming down the stairway from the roof.

WILL EMERSON
We were just grabbing a cigarette on the roof and a very spiffy looking helicopter dive-bombed us and then landed.

JARED COHEN
I know. Come with us. Where's Sam.

WILL EMERSON
I don't know. Do you want all of us>

JARED COHEN
Yes.
JARED ushers the whole group towards the conference room.

INT. OTHER HALLWAY - CONTINUOUS

All five walk in silence. Finally,

JARED COHEN
Just one piece of advice to everyone here before we go in there... this could get a bit ugly but whatever you do... just... tell the truth... don't try to change a word of it, no sugar coating... no one here is smart enough... including the rocket scientist.
He continues on.

INT. ELEVATOR BANK OUTSIDE JARED'S CONFERENCE ROOM -

CONTINUOUS
The guys are taken aback because standing right outside the opening elevator door is a very well dressed page and a female executive assistant who is also dressed perfectly for the day ahead.

ASSISTANT
Mr. Cohen?

JARED COHEN
Yes.

ASSISTANT
This way. They are already in there waiting for you.

JARED COHEN
OK.
INT. CEO'S EXECUTIVE BOARDROOM - CONTINUOUS

They come through glass doors and enter a massive conference room with a commanding view of the city. It is filled with people along one side of the table. There are a team of five lawyers, three compliance officers, a couple of key board members, twelve in all. On the near side of the table sits
RAMESH SHAH surrounded by empty chairs all alone. The head of the table is empty. They all file in and sit down. They all sit in silence... waiting. Finally from a side door JOHN TULD comes walking into the room. He is dressed in a average suit and tie, is not tall, late fifties and doesn't have a hair on his head.
He carries himself without much exception. His eyes however tell a far different tale. Intense even at rest. He walks the length of the room, everyone half stands up.

JOHN TULD
Please sit down.
He then seats himself at the head of the table. Everyone in the room has the printout in front of them. JARED is seated immediately to his left, then SAM, then SARAH, RAMESH, WILL,
PETER, and finally SETH.
JOHN TULD (cont'd)

Welcome everyone. I must apologize for dragging you all here at such an uncommon hour but from what I've been told this matter needs to be handled urgently, so urgently in fact that it probably should have been addressed weeks ago...

(MORE)

JOHN TULD (cont'd) but that is spilt milk under the bridge.
So why doesn't someone please try to explain to me what's the problem here?
Everyone looks around the room a bit and finally JARED speaks up.

JARED COHEN
Well, Mr. Tuld as I mentioned earlier if you look here at the top page of this printout...
He cuts him off.

JOHN TULD
Jared, it's a little early for all that, how bout in English? ... Actually I'd like to hear from the guy who put this thing together... Mr. Sullivan is it?
Does he speak English?

JARED COHEN
Sir?

JOHN TULD
I'd like to speak to the analyst who seems to have stumbled across this mess.

JARED COHEN
Well, that's Peter Sullivan here.
JARED looks down the table to PETER, as does everyone else in the room. JARED gives him a go ahead look.

PETER
Sir.

JOHN TULD
Ah, there he is.

PETER
Yes sir.

JOHN TULD
How old are you Mr. Sullivan?

PETER
I'm twenty-seven sir.

JOHN TULD

Please call me John.

PETER
Yes sir.

JOHN TULD
So Mr. Sullivan why don't you tell me what you think is going on here, and please speak as you might to a young child or a golden retriever, I didn't get here on my brains I can assure you of that.
PETER is very nervous.

PETER
Well, sir. As I guess you may or may not know I work for Mr. Rogers here as an associate in the risk assessment and management office at MBS

JOHN TULD
Now you lost me at M...

PETER
Sorry...

JOHN TULD
I was joking Mr. Sullivan.

PETER
Yes... Well as you probably know over the last 36-40 months the firm has begun packaging new MBS products that combine several different traunches of rating classification in one tradable security.
This has been very profitable as I imagine you noticed.

JOHN TULD
I have.

PETER
Well the firm is currently doing a considerable amount of this business every day. The problem, which is I guess why we are here tonight, is that it takes us... the firm... almost a month to layer these products correctly thereby posing a challenge from a risk management standpoint.

JOHN TULD
And Mr. Sullivan that challenge is?

PETER
We have to hold these assets on our books longer than we might ideally like to.

JOHN TULD
Yes.

PETER
But the key factor is these are essentially just mortgages, so that has allowed us to push
the leverage considerably beyond what you might be willing, or allowed to do in any
other circumstance, thereby pushing the risk profile without raising any red flags.

JOHN TULD
And how far have we pushed that profile tonight Mr. Sullivan?

PETER
We have pushed it to 1.215 Trillion dollars... at MBS alone.

JOHN TULD
Give or take.

PETER
Give or take.

JOHN TULD
Now Mr. Sullivan what I am guessing, and give me a little rope here, what I am guessing
that your report here says is that considering the, shall we say bumpy road, we've been
on the last week or so that the numbers that your brilliant co- workers up the line ahead
of you had come up with in the past don't seem to make much sense anymore
considering what's taking place today?

PETER
Actually not taking place today but what's already taken place over the last two weeks.

JOHN TULD
So what you're saying is it's already happened?

PETER
Sort of.

JOHN TULD
And Mr. Sullivan what does your model say that means for us here?

PETER
Well, that's where it becomes a projection. But...
PETER looks down at JARED for approval to go forward.

JOHN TULD

You're speaking with me Mr. Sullivan.

PETER
Well... sir... if those assets were to decrease by just 25 percent, and remain on our books... well... that loss would be greater than the current market capitalization of this company.
The room goes silent. JOHN TULD looks at PETER long and hard.
He then stands up and goes over to the window and looks into the city.

JOHN TULD
So what you're telling me Mr. Sullivan is that the music appears to be about to stop and we are going to be holding the biggest bag of stinking shit ever assembled in the history of capitalism?
Everyone looks back at PETER.
JOHN TULD (cont'd)
Mr. Sullivan?

PETER
Well sir, I'm not sure I'd put it that way but let me clarify using your analogy, what this model shows is the music, so to speak, just slowing, if the music were to stop, as you put it, then this model would not be even close to that scenario. It would be considerably worse.

JOHN TULD
Well let me tell you something Mr.
Sullivan. Do you want to know why I'm sitting here in this chair with you all, why I get the big bucks, so to speak?

PETER
Yes.

JOHN TULD
I'm here for one reason and one reason only.

JOHN TULD continues to look out over the city for a long beat.
JOHN TULD (cont'd)
I'm here to guess what the music is gonna do a week, month, a year from now. That's it, nothing more....... and I'm afraid... standing here tonight... that I don't hear... a... thing... just silence.
The room falls completely still for at least half a minute.
Then JOHN TULD spins around quickly with a considerably more upbeat tone and looks up and down the table.
JOHN TULD (cont'd)
So, now that we know that the music has stopped, what can we do about it?
Long Silence.

JOHN TULD (cont'd)
Mr. Cohen, Ms. Robertson, I'm afraid this is where you are supposed to step back in.
Lord knows we relied enough on Mr.
Sullivan today.
JARED and SARAH come to attention and gather their thoughts.
JOHN TULD (cont'd)
What have you got for us?
Long pause.
JOHN TULD (cont'd)
What have I told you since the first day you walked into my office? (pause) That there
are three ways to make a living in this business... Be first, be smarter, or cheat. Well I
don't cheat, and even though I like to think we have got some pretty smart people in this
building of the two remaining options, it sure is a hell of alot easier to just be first.
The room goes silent again as Mr. Tuld stares back out the window.

JARED COHEN
Sell it all today...
JOHN TULD smiles just a bit. Then turns.

JOHN TULD
Is that even possible Sam?

SAM looks across the room at JOHN TULD, they have known each other for 35 years.

SAM ROGERS
It is, but at what cost?

JOHN TULD
I'll pay.

SAM ROGERS
Really?
JOHN and SAM look and read each other.

JOHN TULD
I think so.

SAM ROGERS
Almost a trillion bucks of paper?

JOHN TULD
Where does it come back to us?

SAM ROGERS
Everywhere.

JOHN TULD
Sam, I don't think you seem to understand what your boy down here just said... if I made
you... how would you do it?
SAM ROGERS looks down at the table for a long, long, beat.

SAM ROGERS
You bring the traders in for their normal
6:30 meeting and you be honest with them, they're gonna know it's the end either way,
so you'd have to throw them a bone, and a pretty big one. You'd have to come out of the
gate storming... 40 percent done by 10:15 and 70 percent of your positions need to be
gone by eleven, cause by lunch the word will be out. No swaps, no nothing, and by two
o'clock you'll be getting 65 cents on the dollar, if you're lucky, and the feds will be in
here looking up your ass and trying to slow us down.

JOHN TULD
Ramesh?
He looks to RAMESH SHAH down the table.

RAMESH
They'll slow you down but it's yours to sell. They can't stop you.

SAM ROGERS
John... let's just say we pull that off, which is saying something... the real question is...
who are we selling this to?

JOHN TULD
The same people you've been selling this to for the last two years... and whoever else
will buy it.
They look at each other to see if they understand each other.

SAM ROGERS
If you do this you've killed that market for years. It's over.

JOHN TULD
(Nods.)

SAM ROGERS
And you are selling something you know has no value.

JOHN TULD
(cuts him off cold)
We are selling to willing buyers at the current fair market price, so that WE may survive,
Sam.

SAM ROGERS
You'll never sell a thing to any one of them again.

JOHN TULD
I understand.

SAM ROGERS
Do you?

JOHN TULD
Do you!!! This is it, Sam, this is it!
The rest of the table is taken aback and just watching them go at it. Silence.
JOHN TULD (cont'd)
It's 4:00... Jared you've got till 5:00 to break this down and draw me up a plan.

(MORE)

JOHN TULD (cont'd)
Is there anyone else who actually knows what's in there right now, block by block?

PETER
Eric Dale.

JOHN TULD
Where is Eric Dale?

SARAH ROBERTSON
As of today he is no longer with the firm.

JARED COHEN
We have been trying to locate him.

JOHN TULD
So he is just out there with this information?

JARED COHEN
(Nods yes.)
JOHN TULD looks down the lawyer side of the table to a secret service looking guy.

JOHN TULD
Carmelo?

LOUIS CARMELO
Yes.

JOHN TULD

Get me Eric Dale here by 6:30.

LOUIS CARMELO
Done.

JOHN TULD
OK, meet back here in an hour.
Everyone stands up and begins to scatter.
JOHN TULD (cont'd)
Sam... let's talk.
JOHN TULD leads SAM through the back door.

INT. CEO'S ANTEROOM - CONTINUOU
They are now alone looking out over the city as the light from the soon to be rising sun
is starting to show on the horizon. Long silence.

JOHN TULD
Hell of a town isn't it?

SAM ROGERS
Never really did it for me actually.

JOHN TULD
Really?

SAM ROGERS
Always been kinda a grass and tree guy.

JOHN TULD
I've always loved this place. Ever since
I arrived. Everything about it.

SAM ROGERS
I can't say I feel that about anyplace actually.

JOHN TULD
Are you going to be able to come on board here Sam?
They look at each other.

SAM ROGERS
I'm not sure John. This is really ugly.

JOHN TULD
You and I are salesmen Sam, we sell.
That's what we do. It's not complicated.

SAM ROGERS
Exactly. And you damn well know that you don't make a sale unless you think the guy
is gonna come back for more, and tomorrow we are done.
JOHN looks out and then over at SAM and decides whether or not to proceed.

JOHN TULD
This is it Sam.

SAM ROGERS
You keep saying that, what is that supposed to mean?

JOHN TULD
It's the big one. Most of us aren't gonna make it out of this one.

SAM ROGERS
Us?

JOHN TULD
The street.

SAM ROGERS
What are you talking about?

JOHN TULD
This won't be the last `situation' I will be having this week. It's just the start.

SAM ROGERS
It's only the start because we are starting it.

JOHN TULD
Maybe. But I don't think that's true, not this time. The numbers just don't add up
anymore.

SAM ROGERS
Well I agree with you there, I've been saying that for years.

JOHN TULD
I mean if this kid can come up with this...?

SAM ROGERS
I don't think I can go in knowing what I know and put the hammer down on these guys
like this.

JOHN TULD
Oh please, when did you become so soft.

SAM ROGERS
Fuck you soft, you're panicking.
The word panic slaps JOHN TULD in the face. He then calms.

JOHN TULD
If you're the first one out the door Sam, it's not called panicking
JOHN TULD stares aggressively at SAM.

SAM ROGERS
Look, I obviously don't have all the information that you do. But I think this could destroy this firm.

(MORE)
SAM ROGERS (cont'd)
You'll never be trusted again. You are knowingly putting people out of business.
Full stop.
JOHN TULD turns away from SAM and heads over to a phone.

JOHN TULD
You let me take care of that.
SAM heads out the door.

INT. CEO'S GREETING LOUNGE - CONTINUOUS

Sam heads into the hallway where everyone is mingling. He walks over to WILL, PETER, and SETH.

WILL EMERSON
How'd that go?

SAM ROGERS
This is a fucking shit show.

WILL EMERSON
They are going to do it?

SAM ROGERS
Probably.

WILL EMERSON
Jesus.

SAM ROGERS
Remember this day boys, remember this day.
SAM walks out of the room. An assistant comes into the room.

ASSISTANT
Gentlemen, there is some breakfast down the hall if you guys are hungry.
WILL looks at the guys.

WILL EMERSON
Seth, someone is going to have to get breakfast. And let's face it, it's you.

INT. CEO'S TOP FLOOR ELEVATOR BANK - CONTINUOUS

JARED is waiting for the elevator again as SARAH walks up and waits with him in
silence. There is a housekeeping person standing next to them as well. The doors open,
and all three get in.

INT. ELEVATOR - CONTINUOUS

SARAH ROBERTSON
So what's the strategy here?

JARED COHEN
That's where I'm headed right now, downstairs to work on it with my guys.

SARAH ROBERTSON
No, you and I... with Tuld.

JARED COHEN
I'm not sure we need one, Sarah. That's not the way I've ever done this.

SARAH ROBERTSON
(with distinct sarcasm)
Please.

JARED COHEN
He knows where we both have stood on this all along. There's nothing more to do.
This pushes a button with her.

SARAH ROBERTSON
That's exactly my point, and knowing what was discussed by both you and I with him,
I don't see how that can possibly you with anything but a false sense of comfort.

JARED COHEN
I'm not looking for a sense of comfort here, Sarah. I don't think there is one to be found.
The elevator door opens and the housekeeper gets off. Sarah walks after her, but turns
to Tuld first.

SARAH ROBERTSON
So again, what's the strategy here?

JARED COHEN
On this particular front, I'm just not sure there's much left to do.
SARAH looks at him trying to judge the situation.

INT. JARED'S FLOOR ELEVATOR BANK - CONTINUOUS

SARAH holds the door open.

SARAH ROBERTSON
It's very simple. Don't even think of fucking me on this one, because if we are going down... you damn well know its going to be together.
Jared looks at her for a long beat.

JARED COHEN
No, I'm not sure I do know that.
The doors close.

INT. WILL EMERSON'S OFFICE

WILL is sitting at his desk with a large plate of food eating. SETH and PETER are sitting on the couch. SETH is stuffing food in his mouth while PETER eats nothing.

SETH
What do you think Tuld made last year?

PETER
Would you shut the fuck up.
WILL speaks with food in his mouth.

WILL EMERSON
86 mil. in salary and bonus.

PETER
Really?

WILL EMERSON
Yeah, it's public record.

SETH
That's a lot of fucking money.

WILL EMERSON
He was worth a billion.

PETER
Was?

WILL EMERSON
Before today.

SETH
Really?

WILL EMERSON
You'll see.

PETER
....I think I'm going to go get a coffee, does anyone need anything.

WILL EMERSON
(Slight head shake no.)

PETER
I need a little real air.

SETH
Probably a good idea.

PETER
Will, is that alright?

WILL EMERSON
Alright?

PETER
If I get out of here for a minute?

WILL EMERSON
Yeah. Are you kidding? It's not a prison.
Do you want me to hold your hand?
Peter exits. Will's phone rings. Will stares at it and finally picks it up. We only hear his part of the conversation.
WILL EMERSON (cont'd)
Will Emerson...Yes...Oh thank you...I understand...OK.
SAM comes to the door of WILL'S office. He looks at everyone's faces.

SAM ROGERS
What?

WILL EMERSON
That was Eric's wife. He's alive, he's home. He doesn't want to talk to us. And he doesn't
know she called me.
They all look to SAM to see what to do.

SAM ROGERS
Where's he live?

WILL EMERSON
The heights.
SAM ROGERS looks at his watch.

WILL EMERSON (cont'd)
Should we call Tuld's guy?

SAM ROGERS
No... it's Eric... the last thing we need is those guys going over there, you two go try to
get him.
SAM points to WILL and SETH.
SAM ROGERS (cont'd)
But you've got to be back here by 6:00.

WILL EMERSON
OK.
INT. SARAH ROBERTSON'S OFFICE

SARAH is sitting behind her desk looking down at something.
JOHN TULD comes to the door and knocks lightly. She looks up surprised to see him.

JOHN TULD
May I come in?

SARAH ROBERTSON
Please, sit.
JOHN TULD closes the door and sits in front of her desk.
Looks around, then looks right at her.

JOHN TULD
So... we are going to do this thing.

SARAH ROBERTSON
OK.
JOHN TULD
It's going to be tight.

SARAH ROBERTSON
Is Sam on board?

JOHN TULD
Not yet.
TULD pauses.
JOHN TULD (cont'd)
Sarah, I need a head to feed to these traders... and the board... this morning.
SARAH looks up.

SARAH ROBERTSON
Is it me or Cohen?

JOHN TULD
It's you.
They stare at each other, she does not flinch.

SARAH ROBERTSON
Of course you are well aware I filtered several warnings for you and Cohen over a year
ago on this?

JOHN TULD
I'm not sure that's the best path for you to be taking at this point... you're going to be
taken care of here...

SARAH ROBERTSON
(Nods)

JOHN TULD
Obviously it's quite complicated.

SARAH ROBERTSON
John I was told that in no uncertain terms...

JOHN TULD
It was all a very grey area.

SARAH ROBERTSON
It was actually made very clear at the time, by you and I and Cohen.

JOHN TULD
I'd really prefer that you didn't fight me on this...
TULD pauses, they look at each other.
JOHN TULD (cont'd)
We all fucked this one up pretty good...

SARAH ROBERTSON
Yes.

JOHN TULD
We need you to stay here till this is all done and the markets close.

SARAH ROBERTSON
I understand.

JOHN TULD
They'll go over the numbers with you downstairs... Good luck.
JOHN TULD looks at her. There is a security person standing at the door who is waiting for her as he gets up and walks out.

INT. PARKING GARAGE, BASEMENT OF OFFICE BUILDING - NIGHT

WILL and SETH are sitting waiting for WILL'S car to be brought up. As they wait they see JARED COHEN come out of the elevator and walk towards them.

SETH
Ah fuck, it's Jared. He's coming this way.

WILL
What does wonderboy want?
WILL stands up and walks over to JARED.

JARED COHEN
Do you have a minute?

WILL
We're heading to get Eric Dale.

JARED COHEN
I know. I just need a second.
THEY walk away from SETH.

WILL
What is it?

JARED COHEN
Tuld and I have concerns that Sam may not be willing to step up and do the right thing here.
WILL looks around the garage, than back at JARED.

WILL
I don't think that's ever been a problem.

JARED COHEN
Of course it hasn't, but during acute situations, such as this, often what is right can take on multiple interpretations.

They look at each other for a long beat as WILL sizes up the question. In the background the squeals of tires on concrete are heard.

WILL
Sam will step up.

JARED COHEN
I know he will...but if he doesn't...
As the question stands unfinished Will's convertible flies into frame down a ramp and pulls up next to JARED and WILL.
The attendant gets out and before WILL has a chance JARED hands the attendant a tip.
JARED then looks back at WILL who is waiting to get in the car.
JARED COHEN (CONT'D) (cont'd)
But if he doesn't, we need to know that you will.

WILL
That I will what?

JARED COHEN
Step up.
WILL climbs into the car and shuts the door. He looks at
JARED through the open window with SETH now sitting next to him within earshot.

WILL
I have no doubt Sam will make the right choice. And if it makes you feel any better he and I have always had the same interpretation of what's right...no matter how acute the situation.
WILL puts the car in drive and pulls out of the garage leaving JARED standing there.

INT. TRADING FLOOR - MORNING

The floor is totally empty. Slow guitar music playing. The camera glides along the empty floor scanning over the many different empty trading stations and the hundreds of computer screens. It turns the corner and then finally enters SAM'S office.

INT. SAM'S OFFICE - CONTINUOUS

He is totally asleep. He has headphones on and looks like he could be dead he is so passed out. The music suddenly changes pace and the volume change startles him up. He looks around.

He takes the headphones off, music stops. He finally stands up and mildly limps his way out the office

INT. HALLWAY BY TRADING FLOOR BATHROOM - CONTINUOUS
Sam mildly limps down the hallway into the mens room.

INT. TRADING FLOOR MENS ROOM - CONTINUOUS

SAM ROGERS comes across the room and over to the sinks to wash his hands. He looks in the mirror, and then decides to wash his face as well. He stares at himself in the mirror.
The water drips off his face. He looks old. Just then the door opens and JOHN TULD walks into the room. He does not go to use any of the facilities. He stops and looks to talk to

SAM.
JOHN TULD
There he is.

SAM ROGERS
John.
SAM walks over and takes a towel to wipe off his hands and face. Finally he looks up.
SAM ROGERS (cont'd)
So what's it look like John?
The line is delivered a bit too lightly for JOHN TULD'S liking.

JOHN TULD
Cohen has done a nice job. It can work.

SAM ROGERS
What does that mean?

JOHN TULD
It means, as you very well know, that you are a very important piece of this puzzle.
They look directly at each other.
JOHN TULD (cont'd)
Here.
JOHN TULD hands SAM a single piece of folded paper. SAM opens it and looks at it.

SAM ROGERS
That's very generous.

JOHN TULD
It's not a gift. I need to know you are with me on this.

SAM ROGERS
I'm with the firm John.
JOHN TULD is now taking a far more forceful stance, almost blocking the doorway.

JOHN TULD
I won't get what I need out of your boys today unless they believe you... unless they believe in you completely.
He stares at SAM.
JOHN TULD (cont'd)
Are you in?

SAM ROGERS
I told you I have my reservations.

JOHN TULD
Well you can't have any reservations.
They both stare at each other.
JOHN TULD (cont'd)
And I need to know now.
SAM looks down at the floor then at the piece of paper in his hand, then long and hard at JOHN TULD.

SAM ROGERS
I'm with the firm completely John, as I always have been. Excuse me.
SAM slightly moves JOHN out of the way and then he exits, the door closes.

EXT. CITY STREETS - MORNING

There is a haunting blue light bouncing through the buildings. PETER is walking through the streets with mid-size headphones on his ears. The music is all we hear. He wanders around the almost completely empty city and the further he walks the less his face changes.

EXT. CITY STREET - STREET CART - MORNING

PETER finally stops to get a coffee at a small street cart.
He takes off his headphones to pay and the music stops. The wind blows.

COFFEE GUY
One fifty.

PETER
Thank you.
PETER turns around and starts walking but as he looks up he see the figure of a woman coming towards him. It is immediately obvious that he knows her. He stops and she keeps slowly walking towards him. They stop in front of each other squarely.

LUCY
Hey...

PETER
Hi. It's really good to see you.
She has a very sweet face but looks tired. She appears to be a bartender or something, she is not dressed for banking.

LUCY
You too. You look tired.

PETER
I am.

LUCY
What are you doing here?

PETER
I never left work. Just had to get out for a walk.

LUCY
You're still working there?
This cuts him a bit, why wouldn't he be?

PETER
Yes, of course...

LUCY
Oh. I thought...

PETER
How are you? Are you happy? You look happy.

LUCY
I am.

PETER
Well, I should get back... How's your father?

She is pleasantly surprised by this gesture.

LUCY
He's good. Thanks for asking.

PETER
OK. Be safe.
He starts to leave.

LUCY
Hey... You got any inside tips for him?
This stops PETER dead in his tracks. His world tightens yet clarifies. Finally.

PETER
Sell.
She looks at him with concern as he doesn't even hint at a smile as he says this. They then give a small kiss on the cheek, and part.

INT. SARAH ROBERTSON'S OFFICE - DAY

SARAH is sitting at her desk staring out the window. She calmly gets up and walks over to the door and slowly closes it. Then she reaches out and twists the blinds on the glass wall separating her office from the floor giving herself total privacy. She walks over to her desk and sits down. She reaches over and grabs a box of tissues, methodically preparing to cry, almost like a surgeon preparing to work.
She sits at her desk still seemingly calm and collected. Her face starts to tweak just a little, but it just will not give way. Again she tries. And again. She can not cry. She can't believe it. The deeply tragic look of total failure floods her eyes but still hardly a twitch on her face. Still no tears. Finally she makes a forced noise like a sob, but it isn't real and she knows it. Then she tries to laugh to herself, she tries again to laugh, but it too is not real.
She does feel something, but she simply and very sadly can only openly express even to herself... nothing.

I/E. WILL'S CONVERTIBLE - ERIC'S TOWNHOUSE - DAY

WILL and SETH pull up in front of a very nice large townhouse. They both look up at the house dreading going in.

SETH
Jesus, nice place.

WILL EMERSON
He just bought it.

SETH
I hope it was with cash.

WILL EMERSON
You are such a prick, and it wasn't.

SETH
I think I should stay here.

WILL EMERSON
Get out of the fucking car.

SETH
I just don't think it would be appropriate.

WILL EMERSON
Appropriate? Get the fuck out of the car.

SETH
Really?

WILL EMERSON
You're probably right... And don't touch any of the fucking buttons.

EXT. ERIC DALE'S TOWNHOUSE IN BROOKLYN HEIGHTS - DAY

WILL gets out of the car and walks slowly up the stairs. He is about to knock on the door when from behind him he hears
ERIC coming walking up the block. He is still in his work clothes and it looks like it's been a long night.

ERIC
What are you doing here?

WILL EMERSON
Peter finished that model you were working on.

ERIC
Really?

WILL EMERSON
It's created a bit of a shit storm.

ERIC
Yeah, I bet.

WILL EMERSON
Do you want to see it... the model?

ERIC
No.

WILL EMERSON
Really?

ERIC
No. But I'm pretty sure what it says.

WILL EMERSON
Do you think he's right?

ERIC
I'm sure he's right.
They both sit down on the stoop.

WILL EMERSON
Jared Cohen called an emergency meeting of the partners tonight. John Tuld has decided to liquidate our entire position.
ERIC looks over at Will
WILL EMERSON (cont'd)
Today.
ERIC'S face doesn't show much emotion. But he is surprised and sincere.

ERIC
Well, I am very sorry to hear that.

WILL EMERSON
They want me to get you back there, they are worried about you being out here.

ERIC
(with pleasant disgust)
Please.

WILL EMERSON
I'm just saying.

ERIC
(cuts him off cold)
Not a chance.
WILL lets it sit for a few beats.

WILL EMERSON
This is serious shit Eric.

ERIC
You don't think I know that. I've been warning that cunt Robertson about this shit since
last March.

WILL EMERSON
Well...

ERIC
Fuck her... Fuck her.

WILL EMERSON
Look...

ERIC
I signed my papers man, I'm out. They've got nothing on me anymore.

WILL EMERSON
They'll pay...
ERIC looks over at WILL. WILL lets him know with a look that they mean real money.

ERIC
I've already been paid enough by them.
ERIC looks back out onto the empty street.
ERIC (cont'd)
Did you know I built a bridge once?

WILL EMERSON
I'm sorry?

ERIC
A bridge.

WILL EMERSON
No, I didn't.

ERIC
I was an engineer by trade.

WILL EMERSON
Well...

ERIC

It goes from Dilles Bottom, Ohio to
Moundsville West Virginia. It spans 912 feet over the Ohio river. Steel through arch
design. 12,100 people a day use the thing.

(MORE)

ERIC (cont'd)
It cut out 35 miles each way of extra driving to get from Wheeling to New
Martinsville. That's a combined 847,000 miles of driving a day... and 25,410,000 miles
a month and 304,920,000 miles a year saved.
Now ERIC'S mind is racing and he is adding up numbers as he goes.
ERIC (cont'd)
I completed that project in 1986... 22 years ago. Over the life of that one bridge that's 6
billion... 708 million...
240 thousand miles that haven't had to be driven! At let's say... 50 miles an hour that's
134,164,800 hours... or 559,020 days... so that one little bridge has saved the people of
those two communities a combined 1531 years of their lives not wasted in the car... give
or take.

WILL EMERSON
Jesus.

ERIC
One thousand, five hundred, thirty-one years...

WILL EMERSON
Fuck...
They sit and let it sink in.

ERIC
That's what I did.
(beat)
Look... you better get back over there.

WILL EMERSON
Yeah.

ERIC
Crazy shit.

WILL EMERSON
True. Dumping the whole fucking motherload in one day. Fucked up. Well... alright.

ERIC
Thanks for stopping by.

WILL EMERSON
No problem.
WILL looks out down the street as a black towncar comes pulling up to the house.

ERIC
Who the fuck is this?

WILL EMERSON
I'd guess it's the firm's people.

ERIC
What?

WILL EMERSON
Tuld doesn't want any loose ends.

ERIC
They fired me Will. Fuck em... Fuck em.

WILL EMERSON
Just come back with them, take the bonus, and you're home tonight by five. Either that
or they are going to fight you on everything, the package, the options...
ERIC drops his head.
WILL walks down the stairs as the town car stops in front of
Eric's house. The windows are tinted, but they know who it is. WILL walks around to
his car.
WILL EMERSON (cont'd)
You're a better man than I.

ERIC
Well that's always been true.

WILL EMERSON
Yes it has.

ERIC
See ya.
WILL is about to climb in his car.

WILL EMERSON
The house looks great by the way.

ERIC
Thanks.

WILL EMERSON
And Eric...don't beat yourself up too bad over this shit.

ERIC
Yeah.

WILL EMERSON
Who the fuck knows.
ERIC nods.
WILL EMERSON (cont'd)
Some people like driving the long way home.
He gets in his car and drives away.

INT. WILL EMERSON'S CONVERTIBLE - DAY

WILL and SETH are driving slowly towards downtown Manhattan which spans up and out in front of them through the windshield. There is a long silence, and finally.

SETH
So, am I getting fired?

WILL EMERSON
I don't know.
Very long pause, then he looks over at SETH and decides whether to tell the truth.
WILL EMERSON (cont'd)
Probably...yes...almost definitely.

SETH
Are you?

WILL EMERSON
No.
This clearly hits SETH but he recovers quickly.

SETH
Oh.

WILL EMERSON
It's not personal, you're just in the wrong place at the wrong time, the young guys are always the first to go. Nothing
I say is gonna make you feel any better.

SETH
I get it.

SETH looks over at WILL and around at the interior of the luxury car and then back into the city.
SETH (CONT'D) (cont'd)
When did you know this is what you wanted to do?
He thinks that through.

WILL EMERSON
The first time I made 36 million dollars for the firm in the last eleven minutes of the trading day.

SETH
Fuck me.

WILL EMERSON
It was a perfect trade...I saw it coming from three days away. I took my time. I was in, I was out...Pish posh...And it was beautiful.

SETH
How did you learn to do that?

WILL EMERSON
I'm not sure, and whatever it is it could be gone tomorrow.
WILL looks out again at the city then to SETH.
WILL EMERSON (CONT'D) (cont'd)
Look man I'm sorry about this.

SETH
Don't be, you're not doing it to me.

WILL EMERSON
I know...but I'm still sorry. At least you'll have some decent cash to walk away with.

SETH
Only if we can get this done, right?

WILL EMERSON
We'll get it done.

SETH
How?

WILL EMERSON
I'm trying to figure that out right now.

SETH

There aren't really enough willing buyers out there right now.

WILL EMERSON
I'm trying to think of every last one of them I can and then I'll make them willing.
This line sits there for a minute and WILL looks out onto the city.

SETH
Are you ok with that?

WILL EMERSON
I'm about to completely fuck guys I've been doing business with for fifteen years so no
I'm not exactly ok with it.
But look, every last one of them would do the same thing to me in a second...so it is
what it is.

SETH
I guess. And what about everyone else?

WILL EMERSON
Everyone else?

SETH
Normal people.

WILL EMERSON
What are you a socialist? Fuck me Seth.
WILL looks over at SETH, sizing him up, looking to see if he has what it takes.
WILL EMERSON (cont'd)
Look, If you want to do this with your life, and do it well, you need to believe that you
are necessary. And you are. If people want to live like this...with their big cars and these
houses that they haven't even paid for. Then you are necessary. The only reason they
can continue to live like kings is because we've got our fingers on the scale in
THEIR favor. And if I were to take my finger off...

(MORE)

WILL EMERSON (cont'd)
Then the whole world gets really fucking fair, really fucking quickly. And no one wants
that, they say they do...but they don't. They want what we're giving them, but they also
want to play innocent and pretend they have no idea how we get it.
And that's more hypocrisy than I can swallow. So fuck em.
Long look out at the city ahead.
WILL EMERSON (cont'd)
And tomorrow if this all goes south they'll crucify us for being reckless, but if we are
wrong and everything get's back on track. They'll be laughing their arses off at us for
being the biggest bunch of pussies that God ever let through the door.

He is trying to convince himself as much as SETH. They both look out the windows.

SETH
Are we gonna be wrong on this one?
WILL looks into the sea of skyscrapers that now tower above them.

WILL
No...they're all gonna get fucked.

CUT TO:
EXT. STREET LEVEL PLAZA - DAY

PETER is still walking around on the street with the music playing. He crosses a large open windswept corporate plaza.
As he approaches the building he sees SAM ROGERS standing in front having a cigarette. He walks towards him and then finally decides to take off the headphones. The music stops and the wind kicks in.

PETER
Hello.

SAM ROGERS
Peter.
(silence)
You want one?

PETER
I don't smoke.
But PETER holds his place comfortably.

SAM ROGERS
That's good. I don't much either.

PETER
It's kinda beautiful out right now.
They both look out. Slow pacing.

SAM ROGERS
Yeah, I guess it is...
(almost surprised)
I've never really liked this town much.

PETER
How long have you been here?

SAM ROGERS
Forty years.

PETER
I think it's beautiful. The whole place.
Forty years, that's something... Are you tired?

SAM ROGERS
Of What?... Remember I don't work as hard as you do.

PETER
That's not true.

SAM ROGERS
No it is, actually.
Long silence.

PETER
Are we all getting fired after today?
SAM looks out and thinks about it for a while.

SAM ROGERS
Probably.

PETER
They're going to fire you?

SAM ROGERS
That's not what they'll call it,... it'll be a mercy killing really.
SAM looks at PETER.
SAM ROGERS (cont'd)
You don't have to stand out here for me.

PETER
I don't really want to go back in there just yet.

SAM ROGERS
I understand that.
Long beat.

PETER
I think I know your son.

SAM ROGERS
Really?

PETER
Yeah. Not well... but, he always seemed like a nice person.

SAM ROGERS
He is a nice person.
A taxi honks and flies by.
SAM ROGERS (cont'd)
I guess you could say alot worse about a guy.

PETER
Have you told him what's about to happen?
They look at each other to check the nature of the question.

SAM ROGERS
What do you mean?

PETER
This whole thing.

SAM ROGERS
No... I hadn't even thought of it.

PETER
I guess it's illegal anyway?

SAM ROGERS
Yeah... who the fuck knows anymore.... and even if it was you'd sure as hell never get caught.

PETER
He's already pretty rich anyway though right? He doesn't need the help.
SAM ROGERS laughs quietly.

SAM ROGERS
That's very true.

PETER
He works with a friend of mine.

SAM ROGERS
He's a hell of alot richer than me, I know that much.

PETER
But you are taller.

Laughs again.

SAM ROGERS
That's true. It's not much... but it's something... What did your father do?

PETER
He's a doctor.

SAM ROGERS
Really?

PETER
Eyes.

SAM ROGERS
Now that's something.

PETER
Yeah... it is.

SAM ROGERS
Did he want you to do that?

PETER
No, never.

SAM ROGERS
Oh.

PETER
He was always a pretty miserable guy actually...
Another helicopter is heard overhead landing on the building.
Peter looks up.
PETER (cont'd)
They're all coming in now.

SAM ROGERS
Yes they are.

PETER
Have you ever done anything like this before?

SAM ROGERS
No... never.... not even close.
SAM takes a deep drag off his cigarette.

PETER
Oh...

SAM ROGERS
Yeah.
PETER looks down at his watch, then thinks about what to say next.

PETER
Do you really think this is the only... or the... right thing to do?

SAM ROGERS
For who?

PETER
I'm not sure.
Now SAM looks around and thinks.

SAM ROGERS
I'm not either.

PETER
So this is gonna make a pretty big mess of it, then?

SAM ROGERS
I don't even want to think about it.

PETER
Yeah.

SAM ROGERS
Just doesn't quite seem...
Takes another long drag.

PETER
I know.

SAM ROGERS
(Very slightly shakes his head.)

PETER
Well. I guess we should get back.

SAM ROGERS
Yeah.

They both stand in place for a long beat then finally turn and head into the building.

INT. LOBBY ENTRANCE - CONTINUOUS

The camera follows them through the long marble lobby.
Through security. They comfortably don't talk to each other the entire time till they get into the elevator.

INT. ELEVATOR - CONTINUOUS

Staring ahead in silence.

SAM ROGERS
Well good luck, you know, in the future... Seems like you'll probably be just fine.

PETER
Thank you.
The doors open.

FADE TO BLACK.
FADE IN:
INT. EXECUTIVE BATHROOM STALL

A very tight shot of SETH sitting fully clothed on the toilet with the lid on. He is crying very, very intensely but almost silently. He puts his head in his hands and just once or twice lets out a loud noise.

Eventually someone comes into the room and he hears the person go over to the sink and start running water. SETH tries to stop himself from crying. Eventually he accepts that the guy is not leaving and he comes out of the stall and walks over to the sinks. JARED is standing in front of the mirror with his shirt off shaving. His new shirt and tie are on a hanger next to him. SETH walks up to a sink next to him and it is very obvious that he has been crying. He undoes his collar and starts to wash his face. Finally JARED speaks.

JARED COHEN
You alright?
SETH sends him a dagger of a look through the reflection in the mirror.

SETH
You just fired me.

JARED COHEN
I'm sorry...

SETH
This is all I've ever wanted to do.

JARED COHEN
Really?

SETH
Yes...
This hits JARED just a touch.

JARED COHEN
I am sorry.
JARED does up his tie perfectly looks at SETH again in the eye. Then walks out.

INT. EXECUTIVE QUARANTINE ROOM - DAY

SARAH ROBERTSON is sitting in a club chair staring out the window. The coffee table in front of her has a huge spread of fruit and cheese and pastries. She is not eating. She sits and stares. Eventually the door behind her opens, and a
SECURITY GUY walks in with ERIC.

SECURITY GUY
They are almost ready for you Ms.
Robertson. Couple of minutes.
SECURITY GUY leaves the room. ERIC looks over at SARAH then sits in the chair near her. Silence.

ERIC
You as well?

SARAH ROBERTSON
Yes.

ERIC
Jesus.

SARAH ROBERTSON
Yeah.

ERIC
I'm sorry.

SARAH ROBERTSON
Thank you... Sam and the rest of your floor are gone after today as well.

ERIC
Really... and Cohen?

SARAH ROBERTSON
No... still here.

ERIC
Of course...
Long awkward pause. Eric looks around for something, anything to talk about.
ERIC (cont'd)
Are you still dating that tall guy... from the Christmas thing?
She looks over at him with a slight smile, giving him credit for trying to break the ice.

SARAH ROBERTSON
No.

ERIC
He was very tall.

SARAH ROBERTSON
'''......
ERIC
(quietly)
Wow.
Silence.

SARAH ROBERTSON
I did pass on your concerns last year... just so you know.

ERIC
It doesn't matter.

SARAH ROBERTSON
It does.
The door swings open and a catering person comes in rolling a cart with another large tray with more food on it. She places it on the table next to the other food. The abundance is overwhelming.
SARAH ROBERTSON (cont'd)
Thank you.
The caterer leaves. ERIC looks around.

ERIC
Have they taken all the phones out of this room?
SARAH nods yes.
ERIC (cont'd)

Jesus. Paranoid fucks.

SARAH ROBERTSON
Yeah... I didn't think they were going to be able to get you back here.
ERIC stands up and goes over to the window.

ERIC
They told me they were going to drag me through hell on everything from my options
to healthcare over the next two years or I come back and make...
(he looks up and does a little math in his head)
$176,471.00 an hour to sit in this room quietly... it wasn't much of choice.

SARAH ROBERTSON
It never is.
ERIC goes back and sits in the chair.
SARAH ROBERTSON (cont'd)
Obviously looking back, the point was expressed with insufficient urgency...

(MORE)

SARAH ROBERTSON (cont'd) but your point was passed on... I need you to know
that.

ERIC
OK.
SARAH ROBERTSON
Eric.

ERIC
I understand, there was nothing you could do.
Now SARAH questions herself.

SARAH ROBERTSON
I guess... at the time... it didn't seem like there was much of a choice.

ERIC
It never does.
They both look at each other with miniscule smiles, then out the windows onto the city,
defeated. Long silence.

SARAH ROBERTSON
You have kids, yeah?
Long pause as he lets her alone.

ERIC
What is your package going to look like?

SARAH ROBERTSON
I don't know, that's what I'm waiting for now.

ERIC
Should be pretty good, no?

SARAH ROBERTSON
It better be.

FADE IN:
INT. VIP TRADING ROOM - : AM

There are 40 young, 90% male, traders jammed into the conference room next to the trading floor talking very loudly with one another. They are oblivious to what is about to happen. Eventually, SAM, WILL, JARED, and a firm lawyer, come into the room. Everyone quiets down a bit.

WILL EMERSON
Alright, hey...(whistles).
They go silent as they notice SAM standing at the head of the table. JARED and the lawyer are standing off in the corner just to observe. SAM looks somber.

SAM ROGERS
Thank you all for coming in a little early this morning, I know yesterday was pretty bad, I wish I could say that today is going to be less so but that isn't going to be the case. Now I am supposed to read this statement here to you all but how bout you read it on your own time and I'll just tell you what the fuck's going on here.
THE LAWYER looks at JARED then they look at SAM, he continues.
SAM ROGERS (cont'd)
I have spent the night here meeting with the executive committee and the decision has been made to begin to unwind a considerable portion of the firm's holdings in several key asset classes.
The crux of it is... in the firm's thinking the party is over as of this morning. There is going to be considerable turmoil in the markets for the foreseeable future. They believe that it is better to have this turmoil begin with us... as a result the firm has decided to liquidate the majority of its position of fixed income MBS today.
An assistant starts handing out info packets to each of the traders in the room.
SAM ROGERS (cont'd)
You should be getting a breakdown right now, you will see the accounts you are responsible for today. I'm sure it hasn't taken you long to understand the implications of this sale on your relationships with your counterparties and as a result on your careers. I have expressed this reality to the executive committee and they understand. As a result, if you are able to complete a 93% sale of your assets you will receive a
1.4 million dollar one off bonus.

(MORE)

SAM ROGERS (cont'd)
If the floor as a whole is able to achieve a 93% sale we all get an additional 1.3 million a piece. Because of this, if you burn through your allotment by noon, get moving around the floor and start picking up other guys leftovers...
SAM stops for a second and looks around the room.
SAM ROGERS (cont'd)
For those of you who have never been through this before, this is what the beginning of a fire sale looks like. I don't have to tell any of you that the first hour and a half is going to be very important. I want you to hit every bite you can find. Dealers, clients, brokers, and your mother if she's buying...and obviously no swaps, its outgoing only today. This is obviously not the way any of us would like for this to be going down, but the ground is shifting below our feet, and there appears to be no other way out.
SAM looks around the room again, person by person and sees that they indeed know what needs to be done.
SAM ROGERS (cont'd)
Obviously... this is a very unique situation... if we are successful today we will have been successful in destroying our own jobs... I can not promise that each of you will be repositioned within the firm, but I can tell you that I am very proud of the work we have done together here, I have been at this here for 34 years, and I know... from experience people are going to say some nasty stuff about what we have done here, and what you have devoted a portion of your life to. But have faith that in the greater picture our skills have not been wasted, we have accomplished much, and our talents have served some greater good...
He looks down at the ground, then back up around the room.
Then he walks out.

FADE TO BLACK.INT. TRADING FLOOR- : AM

There is a very quiet energy on the floor. A low murmur. Then a hush falls over the floor as people pass on the info that the CEO, JOHN TULD is about to come onto the floor. He appears at one end of the floor and it falls silent. JOHN walks dramatically into the middle of the floor and then into the middle of the row in the dead middle of the floor. He looks around and stands in letting the drama build. Then he climbs up onto the desk and looks out onto the floor like a general.

JOHN TULD
By the end of today almost everyone else in the world, including me, will have considerably less money than they began the day with..... You, in this room, are the exception. You will leave here today richer. You will fire the first shot, I wish it didn't have to be, but at times the market must eat its weak, and you all... are not the weak. We must strike quick, with no doubt, if you hear pause on the line, attack. By noon the SEC is going to be in here getting in your faces, sniffing around, you let us take care of them and you just keep going. We own what we are choosing to sell today and there is

nothing they can do about it. 107 years ago this firm was founded, today we secure our place for next 107.
You've got two minutes before we get started. Let's finish this, so we can get on to the next one...
JOHN TULD climbs down from the table. SAM, who is standing off to the side, walks along the entire floor slowly and then heads into his office.

INT. SAM ROGER'S OFFICE - CONTINUOUS

He shuts his door as the bell rings and his office goes almost silent. Through the glass you see the trading floor go wild, then he walks over to his desk, turns around and stares into the four large computer screens as the charts and graphs begin to move. We just see the back of his head.

INT. INVESTMENT BANK TRADING FLOOR - DAY

Several actual individual trading sequences throughout the day.

INT. SAM ROGER'S OFFICE - : PM

The market has closed. SAM sits, staring at his computers.
There is a knock on his door. He turns and as it opens we hear the sober beginnings of a quiet celebration. He looks up and JARED COHEN is standing in his doorway.

JARED COHEN
Well done.

SAM ROGERS
They did alright.

JARED COHEN
I wanted to give you a heads up. They are going to start sending some people home out here.

SAM ROGERS
Now?

JARED COHEN
(He nods yes) Sorry. No loose ends.

SAM ROGERS
Of course.

JARED COHEN
For what it's worth, you're good... Guess somebody upstairs must really like you.
SAM stands up and walks past JARED without another word.

INT. TRADING FLOOR HALLWAY - DAY

He heads down the hallway and passes the HEATHER and LAUREN
BRATBERG from the opening scene who are returning with boxes to lay off more
people. SAM heads off towards the elevator.

INT. SENIOR EXECUTIVE DINING ROOM   - MOMENTS LATER

The room has ten tables formally set that line a long wall of floor to ceiling windows
with a commanding view of the city beyond. The room is empty except for JOHN
TULD sitting at the last table. TULD looks a little surprised to see SAM but waves him
down. SAM approaches.

JOHN TULD
Sam, please sit. Congratulations are clearly in order.

SAM ROGERS
Our guys did what they could.

JOHN TULD
You did a hell of a job today, and I thank you for it. Sit, excuse me for eating but it's
been a long day. Can I get you anything?

SAM ROGERS
No, no thanks.
They just sit in silence for a long beat as TULD takes a few more bites of his meal.

TULD
So what can I do for you?

SAM ROGERS
I want out.

TULD
I'm sorry?

SAM ROGERS
I'm done, I want out.

TULD
It's been a very difficult day, for everyone.

SAM ROGERS

I need you to release my options, that is if they're still worth anything after today, and I need the bonus. I'm out.

TULD
You'll get the bonus, the options, and keep your current base, but I need you to stay with me for another 24 months. O.K?
They look at each other, SAM seems to know it's not actually a question. SAM is a shell of himself as TULD takes another hearty bite of his meal. He finally looks up.
TULD (cont'd)
For God's sake man put a smile on your face, you did some good today, you said so yourself. I'm starting to feel a little better about this whole thing.
You're one of the luckiest guys in the world, you could've been digging ditches all these years...
SAM pushes back his chair, stands, and prepares to leave.

SAM ROGERS
That's true, and if I had been at least there'd be some holes in the ground to show for it. I'm just not quite sure how we fucked this thing up so badly.
This pushes TULD a bit too far. He also senses he may be losing SAM. He drops his fork, and his tone changes.

TULD
Jesus, when did you start feeling so sorry for yourself, it's unbearable...
What, you think we may have helped put some people out of business today? That it's all just for naught? Well you've been doing that everyday for almost forty years Sam. And if all this is for naught then so is everything else out there.
It's just money, it's made up, a piece of paper with some pictures on it so we don't all kill each other trying to get something to eat. But it's not wrong and it's certainly not any different today than it's ever been. Ever. 1637, 1797,

`  ` `    `   `
, , , , , , , ,
`73, and 1987... God damn did that motherfucker fuck me up good, 92, 97,
2000, and whatever this is gonna be called. They're just the same thing over and over. We can't help ourselves, and you and I can't control it, stop it, slow it, or even ever so slightly alter it...
We just react... and we get paid well for it if we're right... and get left by the side of the road if we're wrong. There's always been and there's always gonna be the same percentage of winners and losers, happy fucks and sad sacks, fat pigs and starving dogs in this world... yes there may be more of us today... but the percentages... they always stay exactly the same.
They stare at each other for a long beat and then TULD looks down and takes another bite. He chews. He looks up again.

SAM ROGERS

I'll do it John, but not because of your little speech, but because I need the money. I'm not sure how it could possibly be after all these years, but I need the money.

They both look at each other again, then look over and see
JARED COHEN walking down the dining room aisle with PETER
SULLIVAN next to him.
SAM ROGERS (cont'd)
You're keeping the kid?

JOHN TULD
Keeping him? He's getting promoted. It's all hands on deck now Sam, there's going to be a lot of money to be made coming out of this mess, we're going to need all the brains we can get around here.
They look at each other one last time then SAM starts walking away and as he passes PETER he just gives him a slight nod.

VERY SLOW FADE TO BLACK:
OVER BLACK:
We hear the sound of someone digging in dirt with a shovel.

FADE IN:
EXT. VERY UPSCALE OLD GROWTH SUBURBAN NYC BACKYARD- : PM
Fade up on SAM ROGERS standing in a hole in the backyard digging. Next to him is a large black medical-looking bag.
He continues to dig. Eventually the flood lights from the house come on and the whole back yard lights up. Then the door opens and a woman in her fifties wearing a bath robe and slippers comes out onto the deck. It is SAM'S EX-WIFE. MARY
ROGERS. She squints towards the back of the yard.

MARY ROGERS
Hello! ... I've called the police.
SAM stops digging and looks up and leans on the shovel handle.

SAM ROGERS
Mary.

MARY ROGERS
Sam?

SAM ROGERS
Yup.

MARY ROGERS
What are you doing?

She comes down off the deck and walks across the lawn up next to the hole.
MARY ROGERS (cont'd)
What are you doing?

SAM ROGERS
Ella died.
MARY looks down and sees the large canine body bag.

MARY ROGERS
Oh God.

SAM ROGERS
Tumor on her liver. It was horrible.

MARY ROGERS
Well I'm very sorry.

SAM ROGERS
Yeah... I really loved that dog

MARY ROGERS
I know, but Sam you don't live here anymore.

SAM ROGERS
I was driving home from the vet and this is the only place I could think to bury her. This
is where she belongs...
She looks at him deeply.

MARY ROGERS
Well. You should have called.

SAM ROGERS
I know.

MARY ROGERS
Are you alright? You look terrible.

SAM ROGERS
Yeah. Tough day all around.

MARY ROGERS
I heard, Sammy called.

SAM ROGERS
Is he alright?

MARY ROGERS
He said they got hammered, but got out alive.

SAM ROGERS
Good, I was going to call him this morning... but...

MARY ROGERS
Well, I am going to go back in to bed.
The alarm is on so don't try to break in.
(Sam smiles)
Well, you take care of yourself.

SAM ROGERS
Is it alright if I finish up here?

MARY ROGERS
Yes.
MARY walks back across the lawn into the house and turns off the lights. SAM starts back in digging the ditch and starts humming a song. He keeps digging as the song he is humming then kicks in with the full version.

FADE TO BLACK.

THE END